beat the moon backwards

where the hogs ate the cabbage
vol 5

Wanda Morrow Clevenger

Writing Knights Press – Cleveland, OH

for Monte,
I have loved you wild

for
the boys
the girls
the grand
babies

beat the moon backwards
Writing Knights Press — Cleveland, Ohio

http://writingknights.com
http://facebook.com/writingknights

All Images by: Wanda Morrow Clevenger
https://www.website

ISBN: 979-8-84565-089-4

Contents

Contents

Contents

Contents

A Winter Wind

During those months he said 'I love you' every day ——twice a day——
as though enunciation of the fragile syllables could indefinitely buoy
time. I knew then we were neck-deep in the in sickness and in health
part of things, one motion short of till death do we part part of things.

And there is plenty of blame to go around. From private insurance
douchery to the fifteen-second-double-booked primary diagnosis –
the copious poisonous child-resistant pharmaceuticals – the emergency
rooms tap dance. The absence of one simple blood test at the onset.

In extreme situations, the brain gallantly tries to save its host
the inconvenience, pulls off that slow-mo car accident trick or post
apocalypse amnesia. In my case, it elected for temporary blackout.
And it is humane to not know and not remember because when
the clouds clear and sight is restored and the view is from the roller
coaster ridge, a winter wind come from out of nowhere, the screaming
you hear next is, of course, all inside your head.

We lost the end of summer and all of fall in 2013. Twenty-eight days
of harvest fell away. He saw to the household chores. Sorted my meds
and needles. He held me when I cried. He said 'I love you' every day
——twice a day——

fear of the dark

at the end edge
they say
your life flashes
before your eyes
but they
are wrong
they are cinematic
writers writing
for climatic
effect

there was
no light or harps
no top-ten greatest hit
countdown
only unconsciousness lit
by pinholes

only squinting deep
inside an ancient cave
where fear of the dark
is really fear
of being eaten alive

horror story

when the twilight
sleep ebbed
held fast to a slab
in Frankenstein's
laboratory of
alarming reason
I silently swore
to never write
of the horror

the gut tube
that looked like
a botched sex-change

what I do
and don't remember

the intubation
the IV
the central line
the catheter
the protracted
protocols

all placed
in fiendish
anticipation

call her sons
they warned
her family
her friends
get them here,
sooner
than later

I'm told I
un-intubated myself
quelled their precious
protocol

so they put
a morphine pump
in my left palm

I remember you
stayed awake
all night
to wake me
when it was time
to squeeze

co-conspirator

one of the
scrubs menagerie
preformed above
and beyond
the nightingale
consortium

in a dark room
of darker thoughts
she sympathized my
other pain, pushed
Benadryl into
my IV toddy

for what it's worth,
she said, and you
probably won't remember
in the morning, you
don't have to tell
anyone what happened
to you

it's nobody's business,
she added, in conspiratorial
whisper

half-assed

when awake finally
in ICU my leg hair
had grown unabated
for 9 days
— —an unsettling umbrage
not seen
since junior-high

all evidence pointed to
felony attempt: blackened
arms & abdomen
ankles bursting their seams
like they'd pound ground
& stuffed me into
cow intestine to cure
over time

& awake finally
life support rigging
was dismantled
& I could
eventually shamble
to the shower room

there wasn't a rail
or a chair &
my body felt alien,
the water beating
off the Saran wrapped
IV disorienting

so I did what I did
in junior-high
swiped the Lady Gillette
half-assed

NPO

branded NPO
for months
then fertilized
liquids only
like a geranium
on its last dry leg

they sucked it
out of me –
the desire
to taste chew
savor
swallow

do or die
they said
sucking the life
out of me

the gatekeeper

meeny miny
moed from glossy
black and white
single-sided brochures
at the check-in counter
he said he was just
the gatekeeper
his job was
to not let anything
get past him

he kept to the script
yes—no
questions—answers
did I want to harm
myself or
others

he divvied out a month's
refill of normality
he was the gatekeeper
his job was to
maintain status quo

it would take
referral to at least
a bi-fold brochure
to get anything
past him

two pills

two pills
one for day
one for night

for a short while
a real coup
using the plastic
gadget that cuts
in two
even if two
was again
needed
and the gadget
not

two pills
a real coup
a pretty bow
a gnarled knot

**necrosis
is a bony bald bitch**

five months into
the pancreatitis
my hair started
falling out

my primary doctor said
rapid weight loss
wasn't to blame, just
stress he said, how
some women will
lose some hair after
giving birth

stress, he said
unconcerned,
while updating
the computer file
while
my pancreas ate
itself

pain

during the 4th hospital wait
&wait&see stint
a specialist was brought in

the guts and glory guy
who takes the big chances
makes the big decisions
painful decisions
who makes no apology
for the chances decisions
pain

one RN around midnight asked,
"are you in any pain?"

only when I cry, I almost said,
but knowing this mattered little
I nodded no

referrals

they sail in
one after another
crisp white sheets
launched from the same
Xerox with
outstretched hand
how are you
hellos

how wasteful
the massed
expertise
made
patient pusher
bean counter

how am I—
surely they see
the paper doll
crumpled
on their
paper sheets

shelf life

the curers
locked me in
4 times in 6 months,
twice on death row—
my crime
fabricated
to fit their
mold
their cure best as
could be billed
before released on
my own recognizance
3March2014
my haunch stamped
with a best-by date

learning center

two gold crucifixes
nestled in the nook
of her throat
the technician at the
diabetes learning
center said
I wasn't depressed
I was grieving

she hesitated, right
hand hovered, as she
asked permission
to touch my arm

we both knew,
the crucifixes
knew,
my loss was
irretrievable
she wanted to hug me
and asked permission
for that too

I could have
told her
– for learning purposes –
the touchy feely
crisscross crucifix
approach
had no impact
on my grief,
the exact opposite
in fact

someday she'd learn
that very thing all
on her own

the 5 stages

a serious young man
was sent to my room
to pick up the pieces

he started in with
the 5 stages:
denial and isolation
anger
bargaining
depression
acceptance

then handed me
his psych card
and left me
wondering
who died

a blacker place

I'm not claiming
that one night
that last admit
I saw the black imps
leap up, a clawed paw
reaching for me
on either side
of the hospital bed,
as if coming
to drag me down
to some far blacker
place than I already
was

I'm only claiming
those hospital admits
were a living hell,
and that I had proof

what worse

complications of
widely worse
such-and-what
that's how it gets you
gets you down
for the count
worms tentacles
in and out
plays Pinochle
on your snout

this is how, then
what worse gets you
isn't the complaint
it's the tentacles

could be argued

it is better
to know what
know what
and
sometimes when,
strip away
bête noire

still, I've stood
there barefoot
on the pier, toes
dangled in the dark
without benefit
of druthers
and could just
as easy went
in my sleep

rogue cords

a sun of teal
and brown calicos
against a tan bee
embroidered
background above
purple deer prancing
through a red forest
resides beside a
porcelain pony
foaled in pacific
japan and a mexican
plumed bird
watching time tick
on a melted merlot
bottle

the composition is
surprisingly symmetrically
complementary

an ice pick in my
left lower gut
jabs at its
irritating discretion

the electrician comes
today to put rogue cords
to code
so when we leave
no one will suspect
anything at all
was amiss

please show interest

sales manager
Mr. John Fan represented
a business vivid
in China for years

a new product of
quality and best price
— — cardboard coffin
boxes by the net — —
raw materials friendly
to the misspelled envirement
best corrugated composite panels
competitive in my
American market

size 210x71x42cm
bearing at least 200 kg
color: cherry, oak, black
and interior decorative material
all custom
as requested

the product replaced
expensive wooden coffins
suitable for burial
and cremation

a gifted pitchman,
how Mr. Fan knew
of my recent brush
with death
was uncanny

he solicited if I might please
show interest of attachments
as he also provided caskets
for pets

nightmare

I like the night
better now
the mad scientists &
maddening hypodermics
are dismissed
& the
monkey see
monkey do
nightmare
is done

the night is gentle
now
I sleep better
now
in my own bed
only knowing dread
of needle days
the east window
can't keep out

Back from the Brink

After the four hospital admits and surgeries, nine months of physical and mental misery, came crawling back a shred of the former me, that retentive bit predisposed to get my house in order — — leave a clean area behind. Same thorough sweep as before vacation departures. Just in case, you know, some freak tragedy occurs and I don't make it back home. Swift removal of real and imagined incriminating evidence.

All thought, action and reaction had been delegated to before and after. Before the shirker, who with unsettling ease said, "We surgeons don't touch the pancreas" and after having escaped his tomb of a thousand tortures.

Paper was easy; what wasn't published turned ash. Bills matched to claims were paid. Get well cards re-read and bundled. Clothes now two sizes too big, boxed. Expired food expelled. Houseplant casualties coaxed back from the brink. Extraneous but billed for nonetheless hospital paraphernalia forcefully disposed of. And with strength regained, cabinets, closets and drawers were emptied one by one, re-organized, and pared down.

I am straining under a new world order, a new lifelong disease. And fear. Fear of medical mishandling and missed good-byes. Of misrepresentation. You know, of not having my house in order when the next freak tragedy occurs.

author's hospital bracelets – circa 2013-2014

blood sugar poem

at 1 short of
three hundred
I hit a wall
roadblocks
blockheads
insomnia
the metal snake
medallion
bouncing here
and there
off a lobster claw
marking me
inferior
infirmed
number conscience
every minute
every day
every night
and there's
no going back
no going on
without
the numbers
and
this poem
might make
it 300

the kind of sick

when Stan died
I missed his memorial
and burial
the tortured words
and sad faces
of old friends,
friends that knew him
better, longer than I

I was sick then
the kind of sick
that doesn't relent
the kind of sick
that binds wrists
to prevent removal
of oxygen masks
the kind of sick
that creeps up like
a hired assassin
the kind of sick
that makes you miss
saying farewell
to a friend
that makes you wonder
why him when
it could so, so easily
had been you

the highs and lows

when the sugars
go high I know
because my head
starts to ache,
and not in a take two
aspirin and four fingers
of Rosé way

the irritant is
just enough
so I know
the innards
are failing
just enough
to cause blank
stares of knowing
stone statues
of knowing the
innards won't
improve
with any practical
resistance
even the cure
has deathly side effects,
I know this from
the fine-print
inserts

the innards
are flailing
sputtering
and it's the
flailing sputter
gives me the
headaches

I read how
human trials
are showing promise
but only for
the long suffering
—step to the back
of the line, ma'am

but the highs
are better than
lows, except
they aren't
in the long run,
the lows are
more dire
in the moment
the highs
a slower slide
south

my endo gives me
a gold star for keeping
my A1C below target

he doesn't know how
I'm doing it
I don't know either

degrees of happy

the NP asked
how I was feeling
with the new meds

much better
I said
I've stopped crying

after four years
at last the cosmos
had cocked its ears
lined the right letters
P. T. S. D.
in the right order

she didn't ask if
I felt happy, only said
she was recommending
medical marijuana

I guessed her at
5 or 6 months along
there's no competing
with that degree
of happy

so it's just as well
she didn't ask

my old skin

I really don't think it's me.
Even though I know it's me.
Who can't get past the past.
Can't crawl over the last hurdle
and into my former skin
the way everyone thinks
I should
—by now.
It's a disease
or symptom
of a disease.
An acronym.
It's a prison
of pain
of grief
of flashes
of unending grief-
induced flashes
circling the drain
but never empting
the sink.
It's going through
the motions.
It's one good flash
in a thousand.
A dry hump
at the kitchen sink.
Me, remembering
my old skin.

flashback flash forward

laying there
awake
in the dark
makes it
ten times
worse

yanked from
dreamfree calm
bedhair peace
no cute kitten
platitude posters
newage
pharmaceuticals
Bobby Flay brunches

just the dark
flashbacks
flash forwards
me
and you

beat the moon
backwards

dawn is hardest
slogged in salted dew
the ticker
tape in my head
on overtime
to beat the moon
backwards
to that instant
before we were flung
too far, before
either of us
was a hamster
on a loop
in fevered wait

10 being the worst

Somewhere between those three days in early December of 1988 and the start of the 2013 pancreatitis horror picture show some graphic design genius added the yellow smiley faces to the hospital "on a scale of 1 to 10, 10 being the worst pain you've ever known, what number would you say your pain is" poster (free advice to all future hospital inmates: the answer is 10. Get the morphine. If you don't need it in that moment, you will need it soon enough). And I could have the timeline wrong since in December of 1988 I was in the birthing wing and having a pain scale facing a Lamaze huffing puffing woman would be an absurd, tacky tack-on to the white board. Could be that smiley face 1 to 10 scale poster has been around as long as the yellow smiley itself. I only can say for certain that the only two times I smiled in a hospital was with babies in my arms.

Are the hospital elite unable to assess pain in the old-school way? Bones gone akimbo, eyeballs rolled into the back of the head, the clutching of chests? The doubled-over-projectile vomiting? Do these elite gain a sick sense of superiority from assessing not your pain but your ability to assess your own pain? Or does it just make their jobs a little bit easier—you know, one less thing.

Every day, every damn day, "on a scale of 1 to 10, 10 being the worst pain you've ever known, what number would you say your pain is?"

10 being the worst (cont)

I tried to focus. Tried to remember the pain of childbirth. Was that the worst pain I'd ever known? When I tripped off the curb on lunch hour in front of Ricchiardi's Clothing on the Carlinville square and my ankle swelled into a black football while I finished out the work day? When I fell off the front porch and face-planted the sidewalk, cracked a cheekbone, two weeks before our son's Maui destination wedding, was that worse? The gallbladder deal, that was genuinely gnarly for a long, long-ass time before they sucked it out of me. But the hundred thousand dollar question is: was it the worst?

At the risk of being ostracized by every medically inclined person I personally do and don't know, pain is pain when it is pain. It's an "in the moment" thing. An apples and oranges thing. And it is my having known a fair share of obligatory pain opinion that the nationally recognized smiley pain scale is a load of hooey. But don't be too surprised if on my deathbed I cave to the hooey and answer "10". Always answer 10. Get the morphine.

how it settles

along a purple stripe hall
you can see yourself
how it settles
in bulged, blank,
darting eyes
hear its jiber

we pass along
quiet as mice
a woman huddled
under heated blankets
repeats one word — — hi
hi - hi - hi - hi -
hi above
a buzzard circles

contribution

a presumptuous thing
a day out
of puberty
who's contribution
to the day
was coordinating
her scrubs
took your vitals
then asked if I believed
in god

you were floating
somewhere
between drugged
and dumbstruck
I was neck deep
between
Rod Sterling
and Edgar Allan

I may have
insulted her
naivety her
inappropriateness
her very presence
in my collapsed universe
but
she asked permission
to pray anyway

I always wanted to title
a poem "road kill"

designated driver
Rob ferries me
daily down
through the river bottom
and back, pointing to
raccoon carcasses

he remarks he needs
some car repairs but
there is no time
for repairs
he remarks he carries
all kinds – little old ladies
bombed bowties
and bridesmaids
chemo patients

back road pundit
hospital hired hand
gentleman to a fault, Rob
jumps out to hold
the car door open

down through the river bottom
and back is 424 miles
I have become
road kill royalty

the Russian

your physiatrist had
a thick Russian accent
and when she spoke
sometimes
her tongue darted
between her lips

no matter what I do
she told me
I should not cry
in front of you

the longer you lingered
thin and weak
it was all I could do
to do what she asked

in time I reasoned
what she asked wasn't
a hard and fast rule but
a rule of thumb
that also applied
to checkout lanes
taxis, elevators and
public privies

Refrigerator Reminder

It's near quarter of six. The pills working in tandem now, I don't wake up three and four times every night . . . or cry as often. Yesterday I woke to a 65 degree house, and with the fan running in the bedroom you can guess how much colder it was in there. I turned the fan off and was still so cold I knew something was wrong. I changed the furnace filter that day and thought I had got the doors shut right—we both know how difficult those doors are—but checked anyway and I had worn light pajamas to bed so was shivering in the far back basement.

The furnace doors were shut even and tight (it wasn't my fault at least) and then I remembered that the thermostat works on batteries and lord knows when they were last changed. But didn't the thing beep or flash a message when the batteries were low? I got the lid off and found some new heavy duty batteries but when that didn't work I took them out and saw a tiny label warning that only Duracell copper top batteries should be used. I found the only two new copper tops in the house and put them in and put the lid back on and nothing happened so took them out and tried the original pair and nothing happened and after switching a couple more times I lost track of which batteries were new and which batteries were original and then started crying. Because that's what I do now.

I was half-crying when I called Dave (Mr. Taxi) and canceled my ride to see you today—he was probably already on the road and I felt bad for that. I'd have to wait another hour before calling Kufa to come out and it was too early for insulin and breakfast so I got dressed and cried and hated that I couldn't remember a day when I didn't cry. Kufa sent a man out within an hour of getting my message and he replaced a small circuit board. The pre-crying me would have commented on how these things only happen in the middle of the night in the middle of winter and we'd both have laughed but nothing is funny anymore. Last time I laughed was when I stumbled onto an internet fart-dubbed video of televangelist Robert Tilton.

Refrigerator Reminder (cont)

I don't laugh at fart jokes. I'm not ten. But this video was truly a work of fart art. Just in case I needed a good laugh, I saved the link but haven't watched again. It takes so much less effort to cry. And I had a dream this morning, the kind that comes on just before you wake up, drifting in and out sleep—hypnopompic, and the thing is I haven't had a dream in a really long time, not one that I remember anyway, and I remembered all of this one. The boys and I and your sister were all sitting at a round table and you were pacing about with a handful of papers (legal farm papers, deeds or something) but your sister didn't look like your sister, she looked like one of the actresses on my soap. She was allied with you over the legal papers. Nate was logically pleading with you to reconsider. Nick was reading from his notes and his phone. I was begging you to listen. You had faraway eyes and couldn't hear us, but you were listening to your sister and when I woke up I wondered why she was in the dream—maybe because when she was alive she stood up for me once. Who knows . . . The whole dream felt hopeless, but aren't dreams suppose to be the worst case scenario so you can wake up relieved it was all only a bad dream.

The day before the furnace fail and the in-and-out dream, a note came from my Aunt Wanda. On three small pieces of pink stationary she wrote how nice and loving and hardworking and kind you were. She wrote of compassion and hopefulness. She wrote of how when I was in the hospital and everyone thought I'd die that you told her I meant everything to you. I sat down and cried all that anyone could ever cry, then stood up and stuck the pink pages to the refrigerator door with a vintage Santa face magnet. It's there among all the other important refrigerator reminders, except it's the only one that is pink and hopeful.

the fare

it took nine days
to wise up
sit in back
wear shades
fake read fake sleep
act like a fare

the driver suffered from
flap jaw: "how many cows
did we have - oh, look
another black dog -
it's suppose to be
nice this weekend
for the Tin Dusters"

the back seat was cold
I was sad, stressed,
sick—my blood sugars
stalled in the 200s

"do you have calves
this time of year - how many
acres - what do you grow -
hey, look, there's a Tin Duster"

he's bored
with the long drive
and sad fare
and he hums
under his breath
aimless notes

sometimes when
I fake sleep
or fake read or real read
he turns on country music
someone's leaving someone
then Christian talk radio
someone's crucifying someone
—I can hear my left eye
inciting mutiny

room number

when I asked you
why you didn't take
my call, you said
you don't like
phone calls, I know
that about you,
you said

I know, I said
I just want to hear
your voice

this isn't my
voice
you said

sonic boom

the calves sold
first thing
the 81 head
ground down
to 18 not much
later, saving
back the two bulls
& the
sentimental mothers

the loss was
a sonic boom
shake rattle &
roll
roll on big wheels
roll me over
in the clover

when you're back
on your feet
we'll truck through
the pasture
like the old days
& watch the
bulls sniff & snort
& climb &
bring it all back
like nothing even
ever happened

November second

against all instinct
a month and 2 days after
you were laid up
way up north
I finally stripped
the bed

I didn't want to
wash the sheets
tuck the corners
line up the log cabins
plump the pillows

was the pills
they dosed up
and dosed out double
that decided

like how your neuro
said what you get is
what you got for as long
as it takes –
he even drew a brain with a bruise
on the patient board
with a face outline

the nose was too pointed
Bob Hope pointed
but his point was made

it was November fall-forward day
I didn't want to fall forward
I didn't want to wash you
from the sheets
but the pills were earning
their keep
and sooner or later someone
would show up unannounced
and find me out

7 am alarm

what one thing was it that
pulled the trigger
you asked

I only knew
what I knew –
med misfires
babes in bedlam
a clanging ghost train
big splintered spoons
stirring and stirring
arsenic stew

pure pain
an instant of
divine silence
thunder of a hundred
rusted hoppers meeting
their maker
rise of krakens
kiss the girls and
make them cry

at the ground zero
7am alarm
I was a disheveled
Peter Falk

I told you I didn't know
about any trigger

3 am cause

those months dragging on
to spare you further anguish
I sobbed to your pillow
of the atrocities
we knew –
preview of new
to come

the furnace cycled on
and off
the sun still afraid
to show its
yellowbelly face

your pillow was soft
and smooth, cool
on my cheek
more than sympathetic
to the 3 am cause

Love note to my husband on 12/13/14

I could smell the hospital's antiseptic agenda when the Administrative Director of Risk Management walked into your room, all smiles. Everyone here is all about the smiles. All about the hellos in the halls. So obviously so, I expect it's the first thing taught the first hour of the first lecture on Day One. Carolyn asked us how was your Thanksgiving and I smiled as much as I can manage in the smile department these days and said, "It was just another Thursday." Her Administrative Director smile didn't waver. I have to give her props for that.

Christmas is looming. A jingle bell bracelet attached to my purse handle jangles when I move from home to taxi to elevator to Room 2429A and back again. Token Christmas cheer—suspiciously similar to the hellos in the halls. This year Christmas will be just another Thursday too and Administration will reappear to check-in with us about this next holiday status.

Since October 1st we've been on countdown to January 5th, when you get the 'all clear' to stand, and walk if your legs and feet cooperate. I'm more a realist than a worrier. I debate at length on how you will feel when sprung from your heinous incarceration. Not immediately, that will be nothing short of elation, but a little later and a lot later and in the middle of the day and middle of the night and when your brain cells kick in every morning. After my four hospital admits for pancreatitis, upon waking was when I got the crushing flashbacks. You'll get them too—and I wish I could but can't say for how long.

Love note to my husband on 12/13/14 (cont)

Strange and unexplainable, the claustrophobia I experienced was phenomenal, though the aversion to music lasted months longer. Dr. Ali said just this week that I had beat the odds, was doing better than he had expected. The antidepressants Dr. Sheedy prescribed took a month to work; the flashbacks are getting foggy.

Did you know that today is 12/13/14? This date won't come back around again for 100 years, so enjoy the factoid for twenty-four because we two won't see this particular sequence again. And it is my constant hope that we won't revisit the past two years again either; no one should have to preview their own fate so exacting. There should be some measure of leniency. The immortals got at least that one right.

labeled

officially labeled
"caregiver" like
this appointment is
some grand godly
gift vastly
improved from
Webster's wife
and mother
and grandmother
that begs
a radical set
of credentials
Lynda Carter's
twin bracelets
a sonogram of
Oak Island
with no option
but to wear sensible
shoes
and tip the Concierge

John

social worker John asked
what was it I thought about
on the long rides up there

he wanted the gory deets
the fill in the down
and dirty blanks

I could tell by how he
leaned back in his chair
he had no better answers
than the rest

nothing at all I said
I stare at the same scenery
or try to sleep but can't

in his entire social worker career
he hadn't come across anything
quite like us, I could tell by
how he leaned back
in his chair
and said nothing

sympathy symptoms

there's a settlement
in our future
that will make
your black lung
money look
like gumball
change
I remind
between the
antidepressant
and Ativan

the side effects
make me queasy
and my legs ache

the first time you
stood, on legs
stripped to the
bone
you puked

it's almost like
you're the pregnant one
and I have sympathy
symptoms

and I'd laugh
and maybe you'd laugh too
if we could

so let's make a pack
I survive
you survive
and we laugh
ourselves
to death

no choice

takes no personal
effort to get here
we phantoms
have no choice in
or out

amounting to more
saying doing more
parting with a shred
of grace
that's the money
shot

but no, we are the
robins the wrens
plowing
beak first into
the same window pane
over over and again
believing we
can see forever

origami

three Christmas'
after everything
went to hell
when I had almost
stopped crying
every day
I learned how
to make
origami stars

the stars were
the first thing
in three years
I had crafted
other than sad
poetry

I made them
with bible pages
and sheet music
an old Rand McNally
to peddle to
the downtown
shops

and like the crying
I couldn't stop
myself
the stars
literally littered
my life

and while the shops
geared up for
Christmas
I couldn't help
but think
everything in my life
had come down to
wishful thinking

recherché redux

a ploy on his part
to purge the
bulldog gloom
with new furniture
neglected repairs
whittling the
wish list
convert to walk-in
lux tile showers same
as in our Maui resort
in March
create a cushy cocoon
for our loitering demise
a faultless vignette
so others can see
we weren't all that
content in mediocrity
a promise
he made to us
to grant every desire
to get back what
was wrongly lost us

so how can one
possibly still feel
glum
birthday suited
in a recherché walk-in
showered with
celadon glass tiles and
the best of intentions

pleasantry

along the hospital corridors
posters encouraged prevention
positivity
pleasantry

please and
thank you

a hundred
thousand
I'm sorry

The Fire

When your back's against the wall, that's when they say you find out what you're made of — how well you walk through the fire — how fast you stand up, dust off and start over and a hundred more pedantic platitudes. True grit and all that burnt-edge fried bologna. But that's what they say. Whoever they are. Or think they are. Or think they know.

But they don't know me.
And even I don't know me. Not anymore.

I do know I'll never grace the cover of Diabetes Digest. I know I'll never write a feel-good, watch me conquer the world, watch me kick ass and take names article that gets my air-brushed sour attitude on the cover of any diabetes magazine. And I'm okay with that. I'm actually more than okay with that.

Just the other day, out of the blue my husband called me "bitter". With the enormity of entangled stank hitting the propellers the past few years, without pressing for a specific it was unclear to what exactly he was referring. How do you pick one out of a thousand miseries to pinpoint where the bitter begins and ends? Or never ends.

Maybe Mr. True Grit has watched too many old western flicks.
Maybe "bitter" is how I walk through the fire.
Maybe I should have informed Rooster of that.

The Fire (cont)

My endocrinologist checks blood test results and A1C readings and cross references a month's worth of numbers and runs the tuning fork test on my feet and says everything is very good. He orders more tests. More bloodletting. More numbers to cross reference. He last asks if anything has changed. I know he is referencing stress-anxiety-depression. These words are embossed on my patient chart as eloquently and permanently as would grace a Victorian wedding invitation.

I say nothing has changed but that I've recently contracted hives and so my numbers are wonky. My endo is at the top of his game. He gets it. He gets me. He says the numbers don't always make sense. He sends me off with scripts for blood work, more appointment dates and a gentlemanly handshake.

To ease my suffering, very early on he told me about a patient who takes 400 units of insulin a day. This bit of endo trivia measured against my measly 32 units makes me one of his less problematic patients—one who could ironically die in her sleep. We both know this. I often wonder about 400 unit guy, if he has given up, if he is bitter. If he feels the fire.

your one phone call

who to dial
with your one
phone call

co-worker
neighbor
lawyer
loved one
ex-love
cab
clergy
cousin twice removed
Long Island Medium
suicide hotline
Giorgio Tsoukalos
Fabio
Guy Fieri
the doctor
the nurse
the lady with
the alligator purse

who would
will drop five
juggled balls
drop mic
at the beckon

how to know
who is left best
to tell you
every little thing
is gonna be
alright

coup de force

because of the
autoimmune thing
I can't take
arthritis meds

those pharms make
my sugars spike
so that's that

while my bones moan
while my blood
threatens a coup de force
I can however have
all the narcotics
I want
doled out
30 per recycle #4
green plastic bottle
least potent up
until I'm addicted
until I'm addicted
and dead

C'est la vie little sister

I've done my research, hitched a ride on the internet information highway the on-rounds residents didn't have time for save where Wiki claims I had to be an alcoholic. (Wiki's prevailing leading cause, the daily resident room tromp had a death grip around that scapegoat's neck.) I read about the mountain of stuff my primary care doc outsources and I read a ton of opinions backed by science and debunked ten ways from Sunday by science—if you're going to put it in writing you gotta pencil in a side door exit.

Sure, I cry every day. Going on three years come mid-August if you don't count that first ICU unconscious stretch in never-neverland. Nitty gritty: only so much pain and fear can be inflicted on a person before they crack.

On any given day my symptoms line up with PTSD, anxiety disorder, grief and a paralyzing I know what will kill me disengage. I'm the woman on the TV commercial whom upon meeting an acquaintance in the grocery aisle holds a smiley face mask up to hide her "been to hell and back" face. I'm the woman who went from Southern Baptist to agnostic to "give me an effing break."

It's a chronic disease they fumbled around and left me with. Granted, something horribly wrong had occurred with my immune system but still, the lot of them (I still see their inept faces) had fumbled around for nine months with little to no expectation that I would survive—efficiently sealing my fate. The torture touted as medicine goes without saying. Just my luck to live in the wrong time in the wrong place with the wrong doctors. C'est la vie little sister.

Type 1 diabetes complications (with an MIA pancreas) are long as my leg. And it's a certainty if one don't take you out, another will. The odds of me succumbing to drowning, cliff fall, plane crash, tied to a train track, falling piano, ten car pileup, shot, shanked, bludgeoned, poisoned, choked, or while saving Private Ryan pale by comparison.

So what if I cry every day. So what if I've kicked god to the curb. I've done my research. I know what will kill me. If it doesn't blind and maim first.

This isn't a suicide note, but you can borrow it if you want

I'm just saying, neither of us should draw breath. If all had gone as expected we'd be the terminally late to supper Mr. and Mrs. And for the record, I don't want to be pickled, put on display and locked in a box six feet under. Cemeteries are for ghouls and the over-eyelined Goths. But that whole pod-people that compost and grow into a tree is too god-awful ghoulish too. Yeah boy, bury Ma and Pa Pod in the back yard and wait for something to come creeping out of the sod. You're gonna have to hire a backhoe for the job, get all kinds of government permits and with the compost pod prep you won't save any money in the long run, son. Death is Wall Street—they're lining up to wrangle what's left out of your blue fingers. Nope, put my ashes in a wind chime, one that isn't too tinny or clangy and hang it in a normal tree. One from the nursery that flowers. One with squirrels.

And just because we're breathing and the kitchen clock is ticking and the laundry is sloshing and I'm typing, don't think either of us beat the odds; the two aren't necessarily attached at the liver. Odds are just that, what you're left with when the doctors are in way over their skill set.

This isn't a suicide note,
but you can borrow it if you want (cont)

I'm sick to death (pun intended if you want) of the doctors saying I beat the odds while shaking their baffled heads ever so noticeably. I know they're thinking one in a million effing lucky old broad, or worse, some kind of miracle (which truly pisses me off). There were no miracles. Not in my hospital rooms. Not in his. Pure putrefied cause and effect.

In my case, since there was no wage loss I was worth more dead than alive.

In his case, a signature was required to guarantee we'll never tell the truth. The whole truth. The putrefied cause and effect truth.

No, this isn't a suicide note. Don't anyone panic and order a Magnolia. I'm not planning on swallowing a bottle of Ativan because I'm told I'm worth more dead than alive. That's something I should've suspected from the start.

altered states

one of the side effects
of the new med
is vivid dreams
epic altered states
of identity nightly
doomsday drama
apocalyptic scenarios
of altered survival
that fade quickly
upon waking, taking
with them any hope
of foretelling

but it doesn't matter
anyway
when doomsday comes
however it comes
those wounded of us
who take the meds,
any meds, all the meds
will be the first to fall

two years ago

too much damage
for far too long
we got it in our heads
to take a powder
dissolve into
witness protection
start over
the new old kids
on the block

we put down earnest money
two states away
then panicked and pulled out
the next day

he didn't want to leave
all he ever knew
I couldn't survive
any more damage

that was two years ago
a red suit is in office
despite Illinois decked
out in denim

the farmers around here
still gripe when it rains
and
when it doesn't

we all fall down

you might think
the worst is
the enormous effort
to push off the bedspread
and put your feet to the floor,
the blank slog
to the pill bottles,
the first glucose
number of the day,
and the next
and the next,
the never knowing
if it's a good day
or a bad day,
if the rug you ordered
off Overstock
is too red or
not red enough,
if you'll ever
summon the
almighty will
to show up
to open mic night
again,
not knowing who
will survive who
but suspecting
a high hard tide
less in your favor,
the falling face-down
again and again,
the crying jags

but the worst is
the rampant
oblivious chirping
out every window

heavy laid lull

in the jet lull
the rippled jet
the one mississippi
two tick
a boulder
laid chest deep
knows nothing
of the strangled
heart

the soul asks
only for heavy
laid lull
and mississippi
tick jet

things could be worse

more and more
I think on how
far is too far
how much
too much
at what point
is pinpointed
where the hogs
ate the cabbage
and
how satisfying
it would feel
to scoop up
all the things
could be worse
happy half-fulls
and hurl that
unfailing
optimism
at the closest
brick wall
to see it
flail the air
then splatter
drip and drain
to the ground
left empty
to evaporate
completely
between glass shards
to show
unequivocally
what worse
looks like

antivenin

we milked
all that venom
from cells, texts,
landlines, e-rants,
pm's, those
hostile
close encounters
and violent
telepathy
and found
there was enough
serum
to save our
heinous souls
even to
the final strikes

Wanda Morrow Clevenger wrote eight poems in a handful of months in 1974; thirty-four years later she returned to writing. She has since placed over 467 pieces of work in 158 print and electronic literary journals and anthologies.

In August of 2013, while compiling the manuscript for this book she fell ill with pancreatitis, further complicated by necrosis in the following nine months, and wasn't expected to survive. One year later, almost to the day, she sat down to finish *where the hogs ate the cabbage.*

She has her husband to thank for the title.

www.ingramcontent.com/pod-product-compliance
Lightning Source LLC
Chambersburg PA
CBHW071455150726
48000CB00006B/2561